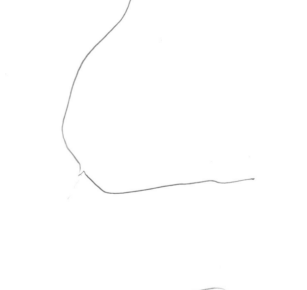

TRULY, WE BOTH LOVED BEAUTY DEARLY!

The Story of
SLEEPING BEAUTY

as Told by
THE GOOD AND BAD FAIRIES

by Trisha Speed Shaskan

illustrated by Amit Tayal

PICTURE WINDOW BOOKS
a capstone imprint

Special thanks to our adviser, Terry Flaherty, PhD, Professor of English,
Minnesota State University, Mankato, for his expertise.

⁘⁘⁘

Editor: Jill Kalz
Designer: Lori Bye
Art Director: Nathan Gassman
Production Specialist: Kathy McColley
The illustrations in this book were created digitally.

⁘⁘⁘

Picture Window Books
1710 Roe Crest Drive
North Mankato, MN 56003
www.capstonepub.com

Library of Congress Cataloging-in-Publication Data
Cataloging-in-publication information is on file with the Library of Congress.
ISBN 978-1-4048-7940-9 (library binding)
ISBN 978-1-4795-1945-3 (paper over board)
ISBN 978-1-4795-1949-1 (paperback)
ISBN 978-1-4795-1883-8 (eBook PDF)

Printed in the United States of
America in Stevens Point, Wisconsin.
032013   007227WZF13

People around here call me the Bad Fairy, or "BF." My real name is Edna. I'm the one who cast that spell on Sleeping Beauty. That's not the whole story, though. The story begins before Beauty was born, when BF used to mean something different.

I'm Edna's younger sister. I'm the so-called Good Fairy, otherwise known as Stella. You can't count on my sister for the whole story. I'm the one who knows it all.

Pish posh, Stella! I'm more than 500 years old. I'M the one who knows it all. Now let me tell the story, please. I first met the king long ago. We became friends, and he named me his BF (which stood for "Best Fairy" back then). I bewitched his castle. It still sparkles to this day.

Yes, Edna was once the king's BF. But over time, her mind got a little rusty. During one Lunar Festival, Edna overdid it and made the moon glow too brightly. It nearly blinded everyone. I told her to stop.

"Moonlight," Edna said, "time to drop!"
(She was supposed to say, "Time to STOP!")

6

The moon dropped. Fast!

After that, Edna wasn't invited to anything. It was just too dangerous to have her around.

One day the king and queen announced the biggest party ever: a feast for their new baby girl, the princess. All the fairies, except Edna, were invited. Each of us prepared a special gift. I worked on Gracefulness (because, you know, a princess shouldn't be klutzy).

I did NOT get invited to the feast. A mistake, surely. The king wouldn't forget his BF, would he? So I prepared my gift for the princess: Compassion. Every princess needs the ability to feel and understand the troubles of her people, right?

On the day of the feast, the guard checked the guest list. I wasn't on it.

I had never felt so bad in all my life.

I loved the princess dearly, and I was going to give her my gift—with or without an invitation.

So I fired up my wings and flew in through a window. Stella was just about to give her gift of Gracefulness.

"On the princess' 16th birthday," I shouted, "she will prick her finger on a magic spinning wheel! The wound will stand for the suffering of the people of her kingdom! And it will remind the princess to be kind!"

Edna's spell began well enough. But then she said, "Don't worry, dear princess. When you die, your tears will comfort lives!"

(She was supposed to say, "When you CRY!")

I don't have Edna's ancient powers. But I did my best to fix the mess. My NEW gift to the princess was that she WOULDN'T die on her 16th birthday. Instead, she would prick her finger and fall asleep for 100 years.

When I mixed up the spell, the king banned me from the castle. I didn't have a chance to fix my mistake. So I waited. On the princess' 16th birthday, I dressed up as an old woman. I snuck into the tower and spun the magic wheel myself. That way the princess wouldn't do it, and we could avoid the whole sleeping-for-100-years mess.

I knew Edna was up to something, so I followed her.
Her plan began OK. But then the princess walked in.
She'd seen a light in the tower.

"Go away!" Edna yelled.

But it was too late. The princess
had already stumbled and pricked
her finger. What a klutz.

15

I did the only thing I could do: I put the entire castle to sleep. Vines grew and spread. They covered the walls and the tower where the princess slept.

For years everyone snoozed. Over time, word traveled of the lovely "Sleeping Beauty." (Fairies checked in on her, you know.) Many princes tried to climb the tower. None had any luck.

I felt dreadful and stayed far, far away. I didn't want to make things worse. But how much worse could they get?

Finally I decided I HAD to make things right. I dressed up as an old woman again and returned to the castle. A prince entered the castle grounds. I waved my wand and chanted:

"Compassion is the fullest of gifts. Compassion will bless you and your lips."

The vines fell off the tower. The prince ran up the stairs.

Stella (who was spying on me again) flew up with me just in time to see the prince kiss the princess. At that moment, the castle sparkled. Everyone woke.

No one, except my sister, ever knew I was the one who broke the spell. People still call me the Bad Fairy. But that's OK. I was happy to hear the prince and princess had a lovely wedding. And I'm already working on a gift for THEIR new baby girl!

Critical Thinking Using the Common Core

Look online to find the original story. Describe how the "Bad Fairy" character looks and acts. Compare and contrast that Bad Fairy with the Bad Fairy (Edna) in this version of the story. (Integration of Knowledge and Ideas)

If Sleeping Beauty told the story instead of the fairy sisters, how would her point of view differ? What details might she tell differently? What parts of the story wouldn't she be able to tell? (Craft and Structure)

Edna, the Bad Fairy, isn't really bad in this version of the story. She just makes a lot of mistakes. Describe her blunders, then list the steps she takes to correct them. What role does her sister, Stella, play in the story? (Key Ideas and Details)

Glossary

character—a person, animal, or creature in a story
point of view—a way of looking at something
version—an account of something from a certain point of view

Read More

Casey, Jo, Beth Landis Hester, and Catherine Saunders. *The Princess Encyclopedia*. Disney Princess. New York: DK, 2010.

Piumini, Roberto, retold by. *Sleeping Beauty*. Storybook Classics. Mankato, Minn.: Picture Window Books, 2011.

Wilcox, Leah. *Waking Beauty*. New York: G.P. Putnams Sons, 2008.

Internet Sites

FactHound offers a safe, fun way to find Internet sites related to this book. All of the sites on FactHound have been researched by our staff.

Here's all you do:
Visit *www.facthound.com*
Type in this code: 9781404879409

Look for all the books in the series:

Believe Me, Goldilocks Rocks!
Frankly, I Never Wanted to Kiss Anybody!
Honestly, Red Riding Hood Was Rotten!
No Kidding, Mermaids Are a Joke!
No Lie, I Acted Like a Beast!

Really, Rapunzel Needed a Haircut!
Seriously, Cinderella Is SO Annoying!
Seriously, Snow White Was SO Forgetful!
Truly, We Both Loved Beauty Dearly!
Trust Me, Jack's Beanstalk Stinks!

Super-cool stuff! Check out projects, games and lots more at www.capstonekids.com